Date Due

for Samantha and Vanessa with love

There was a child named Bernadette
I heard the story long ago
she saw the Queen of heaven once
and kept the vision in her soul
                    –Leonard Cohen

LOVE
AND OTHER THINGS
THAT HURT

D.C. Reid

Black Moss Press
1999

Published by Black Moss Press 2450 Byng Road, Windsor, Ontario
N8W 3E8

Black Moss books are distributed in Canada and the U.S. by Firefly Books,
3680 Victoria Park Ave., Willowdale, Ontario, Canada M2H 3K1.

Black Moss Press would like to acknowledge the generous support given by
the Canada Council for the Arts for our publishing program.

CANADIAN CATALOGUING IN PUBLICATION DATA
Reid, D. C. (Dennis C.) 1952–
    Love and other things that hurt

Poems
ISBN 0-88753-328-0

1. Title
P8586.E4486L68 1999 C811'.54 C99-900728-9
PR9199.3.R44L6 1999

Published in Canada.

Table of Contents

Paper Heart

My Daughter And The Rest Of It

Designing The Perfect Woman

Love And Other Things That Hurt

Paper Heart

...no one believed what she had seen
no one believed what she heard
that there were sorrows to be healed
and mercy, mercy in this world

—LC

The Only Perfume

In Japan, a monk rakes sand round rocks all day.
They are mountains rising through cloud,
       a gesture of hands, sorrows being healed.
His ritual preserves and signifies.

Mine is the bare hand on a ring of fire.
Each night I pull the drapes and feed the cat,
       close the basement door.
I place my own bare hand on the stove, don't trust my eyes.
         Fred's daughter taught me this.

In this dusk that hangs, something takes hold of me
       perfect as a child.
It's the only perfume, sea air closing over me.

Is this the smell of everything,
           of flotsam and dissolution?
Is this the pull of instinct
        though we're free to choose?
Sometimes I burn.

Sometimes this blend of yearning surrounds the summer dark with its
     smell of freedom.
The world I inhabit is a blue-green gem in the moist dark mouth of night,
       the long travail of gravity, tending an unimportant
                 corner of the sky.

Fred secured his domain in ratty slippers.
I mount the stairs in dying light, lower my hand
       through guywires of the universe.

She Wants Her Father Back

Sitting in her warm bath,
she pulls the razor and weeps.

From her small plastic bathcap0
a Borneo tribeswoman stares out.
She sits in our white tub in her white face

from a white jar and hurts my eyes.
She is far, far away drawing her slick razor
through delicate, lemon-lime cream.

Her leg emerges from Papua New Guinea.
Where are the flames? The grease-coated bodies
dancing on walls?

Her arm pulls evening up her thigh.
I wait with my kleenex, between pity and rage.

I understand it is not me she wants, not my fault,

                                  not my place
to come inside, but days turn into years
and still she wants her father back.

                        There is nothing I can do
                        but watch the blade.

Standing In The Doorway

Standing in the doorway,
Sammy knows the family eating disease
has come for us.

I steal her being young.
I make her clairvoyant,
make her eyeballs stand on end.

All she's known is war,
the pibloctu scream
of an iceberg letting go.

There should be amber, a pimply boy for her,
greedy lips that would kiss their way to love.
Not this. Not this.

Numbness is a howitzer, brown-eyed shame.
Hear the silence at the end of a marriage,
the casualties. How it radiates. How it infects.
How they drop like plums.

She takes the big pill.
Her head is near the roof
stuffed with Shakespearian weather.

Thinking bulges in her eyes.
Tears freeze like thumbtacks.

I am a thief to make her well. I would be God.

Paper Heart

Head at my rib,
handing across her paper heart, pink
to glue a family together.

8 years old,
a collection of 200 pliable bones,
small metacarpals pressed to the back
of my hand.

Divorce is bone dust
in ribs of sun from venetian blinds
laid across her bright eyes.

Wind and agony are invisible,
the dissection of a marriage,
the spurt of disjecta membra.

A butcher knife would be a blessing,
blood in gutters, carcasses
hung like weird dolls.

Behind doors, food in its freshness rots,

Vanessa's fragile skull with its net of veins.
The inverted retina of an eagle
sees far but does not cry. Lucky bird.

March 26, 1994, ordinary,
lethal with shame.

Her paper heart strips off
and I press it back, hopeless,

weep uselessly against the fridge, pour
orange juice on the floor.

Hold Me

The weeping when nothing comes out
says hold me.

The green earth in its envelope of air
says never let me go.

Me in my nakedness
mouth, I be strong don't I?

The ceiling has cerebral palsy,
my limbs twitch like useless vegetables,

and Vanessa
shivers in my arms,
hiccupping in the news. Divorce
has penetrated the voluptuous flower
of the cerebrum I have betrayed.

Continents are ripping free, constellations in the sky.
Hold me   hold me   hold me   hold me   hold me.

The best thing to do with pain is take it

from the flesh because it has no armour

from the swallow because it offers perfect flight

from the blue-green earth because it lives so far away

from the sky because it asks nothing

from all the beings in all the next dimensions and from all their brethren

from my child because she is deciding against me

from my heart

       because I have nothing to give or receive,

and give it to that woman. Fill her full and polished as a chestnut,
          and one more thing. Grant her the life without an end.

He Considers

the compliant knife, the scissors, the docile spike ...
all implements of death in the wrong hands.

But how to choose?

How to recognize the hands, I mean.

On The Dock The Railing Fades

The boat moves within its hum toward another shore.
Mist is in the reedyness and all day the sea is waking.

    A bird
in following the sun flies only to death
           and the boat is near that place.

I tell myself it's Sunday and I've had a few beers.
The ripple of fear
        moves clear of madness,
folds over until it's gone.
           Leaves me the wake inching closer,
flesh and blood returning.

I Love My Family

One year after disintegration,
the body of a family
becomes ribcage, skull, rising through

soil in some forgotten farmer's field.
The note arrives,
pinned to the most ordinary fridge:

I love my family.

Nine years old
and the message follows her paper heart,
her assurance in the solidity of things,

the necessity of mother, father,
the older sister who finds puberty
a thing too hard.

A second shadow she is to me,
head in the hollow above my hipbone,
doing homework on the couch

before a fire that may be the only one left.
She ruptures my convalescence
with guilt, he who pulled the plug.

She loves her family, and I do too.
I would gather the bones

of murdered relatives
and hate until death,
the brown-eyed traitor

who stuffed their bones behind the furnace.
But she pokes out.
how she rises
her smile lifting through

to me

that scribbled heart of hers,
one step always and only

ahead of despair.

My Daughter And The Rest Of It

...so many hearts I find
broke like yours and mine
torn by what we've done and can't undo
I just want to hold you
won't you let me hold you
like Bernadette would do

       –LC

Always Leaning Through The Edge Of Myself And Feeling Nowhere

How when daytime comes to extinguish the night do we know the moment,
     do we say, now, now we are
               completely changed;

the time Samantha ate a mouthful of guitar and I slept with her in the hospital,
     folded to a linoleum chair; the wall where my head kept hitting
I would later decide to call a pillow.

Through a nearby window of the past, a child's face, black eyed, intent,
       and the surprise that it is my own, or a face much as my own:

     the child, not a man or woman just yet,
   discovering the shock of the first orgasm, and coming back from that place,
becoming a thing again, sentient, then the smell of lemon oil, the dusty piano.

How then the body lies open-handed in the indolence and beauty of perfect sleep.

For me, the problem in all this well-phrased nostalgia is this: real life,
and it is always rushing towards me, like a wasp
the more it is pushed away.
           Truly, I confess it, I came of age in an oxbow.
I had walked into the foothills and taken off my clothes. Warm mud, intricate
with trails of insects.
         There is no other English for I fucked it and I fucked it,
and found no relief; what boys are reduced to in the time before women.

   When her time would wait no more, Samantha left a tampax wrapped in tissue,
a little bun
   on the windowledge. The bathroom
          with the smell of steeped blood behind the door.

Then the way a human person becomes aware of himself when he is being watched.
I looked up from my spent poem to a cliff which will always be there but also here.
There I find the horse on two thick legs fingered with veins.

Then the eye of the horse, a flash of judgment, blue and deadly
as the pools where old plutonium decays.

I pull my muddy penis from all that's beneath me. My daughter flies right through
me, her wild corona of hair or mane, call it what you will.
And the memory is seared by this light that finds the crack in things.

So the old fear or shame is once more upon me, I am no longer certain of the term,
the knowing there is no one I can turn to and ask, am I a man?

SURELY ALL ART IS THE RESULT OF ONE'S HAVING BEEN IN DANGER, OF HAVING GONE THROUGH AN EXPERIENCE ALL THE WAY TO THE END.

- Carolyn Forché

"The poem doesn't happen this way," she says and paints a lighthouse
     that isn't there.

"One rearrangement of living is art," I say and squeeze the perch until it bleeds.

There is no danger as her leg blurs in the water off the dock, that world
     before man and paint, her calf within which razors could sink
          like a necklace. Then the fronds of blood.

"Another," I say, "is memory, the dominion of the past." I could write a straw hat,
     word the light that marks a landscape France.

But fish blood drops to the surface of another world
     sharks apprehend in parts per million, and the ocean fills
          and releases the shore like a beautiful species of sex.

"All other is surrender to the arbitrary, the accidental," say I; marvellous the ease
with which reality
          caves in to the palette,
               the way a building, explosives set just so,
        collapses among the others.

And the float upon which we float is not the ground.
Her bent-up calf returns as though having passed into a milder realm
where the gentle removing of flesh from bones is a reverence.

The lighthouse rises, white upon white. Sammy loads her wand with red.
        And now the shark comes curving,
      eery and prehistoric, from out of its shadows.

And here is her leg, and here, the answer to the obvious question.

"I don't do people ... something about the hands."

To fish for sharks, I think, the perch is slit from vent to gills and turned out
        like a glove.
Afternoon under the yellow sky on a wharf named Lothlorien ends
with the reel giving ground, a rod
                            bent under a mystery, fierce,
              and capricious, invisible.

When Come Adults In A World Where There Are Only Children

How swaggering and brilliant that January 16th in glass light.
Her mother and I plundering one another on a bare mattress.

And then the legacy:
the grotesquery of broken bones, of forceps, blood

finding its quiet ropey way to drain from a vagina.
Is it monotony that makes the eye cry out for less?

Sammy's flattened face on my hand, the knowledge
my unaccountable life was at an end.

And then there is the title, the way it may focus a poem
through the years a poem lasts, and rain

the greening yard, until they ache with clarity.

I might remark *California poppies* along the path.
She would not see them, so ferocious in their orange suits.

I might single out flowers. Hydrangea might bloom
        through the bodies of mice, lifting
pale bones through the delicate strains of rain.

But what are they lifting? And for whom do they bloom
if Sammy brushes by on a hurry toward her future,
rolling eyes at my gormless clothes?

When come adults in a world where there are only children?
How can I ask this thing anymore?

She says nothing and it rises like a wall,
lounges at the slatted gate in her tartan skirt,
Oxford shirt gone scrunchy at the waist,

this teenager in her present, hair so black its blue.

24

She might cease walking upon the cracked concrete path
and become invisible for all my looking.

In a bolder self I might retrieve her. *Mouseribs* I'd say.
Only a delicacy opened toward us as an adjective of death.

Come look I'd say. But there's no time. None.

Why I Can Breathe On The Mirror And Disappear

The way a man drops at Passchendale, at Omaha his life a red antler out his
    head.
        Bodies on barbed wire frozen so patiently, their hands,
            in the long wind, clinking like glass.

Much east of here someone has already saved the world this morning.
        And others before it.

I stood among pale ribs in the shadows. My own and those before me.
        And ripped apart their basement.

As if an address could rescue anything.

In creating a home for someone else to fill up with their lives,
        I found a mummified bandaid, scabs of Donna Reid, a copper bell
never used anywhere but in a child's game. Left with intention between walls,
    in the dead space
of a forest shaped into the bones of a house. How odd my hand on glass but
    not on any thing.

I unearthed the names of boys cut with a pen knife. Eric and William.
        43 years ago when the world resumed again,
                when allied cities swelled with babies,

with addresses, small houses. 1539 Davie St.

Petunias lushed the plaster and lathe, easy trumpets, loud and unremarkable.

Après la guerre.

The History Of Housebuilding

Listening to December. A gust of piano lifts invisibly from the stairwell,
the blue flap of her duffle coat, the careless beauty
        of a school girl's arm of books:

these are what hope is made of:
2 x 4s sweet and nailed within their walls.

If you loved me, you wouldn't have left my mother.

Breaking holes in the wall I find nothing, and then more nothing,
Fifty years of dust falling into itself
                        and the cold sound of January
resuming. Storm light. Passing like emotions across a
        new-born face.

If you loved me, I'd clean up the suite and have my friends over.

She would come and go by the same white door, the four white appliances
purring their pure anonymy. The walls I fill with fibreglass.

In a time withheld from us: a girl at play in a crown of bent branches,
a future in apogee she has not yet assumed but owns more

actually than the Doc Martins buckled upon her feet.
I think I hear my daughter

singing in a voice that comes from somewhere else.

If only you loved me...

A windowsill of tipsy flowers reaches for the one vital word.

What I'd Pay For Freedom

How to achieve a sense of starting

                when the images won't leave me:

the children of Africa

          too listless to sweep the flies from their eyeballs.

And something about the wind, bending the trees into faces, now miracle,

     now awful,

        a wading pool lifted out of our lives and taken

             to a further place.

Even money isn't right. In a fall without security, I gamble

with all my income:

      You say you'll give me a suite for free but you really want my sister.

How to continue when October is a presence thrown into the sky,

       long hair blown across Sammy's face, held by the persistence of roots?

This is finally my real life: being haunted. Then leaning into it

                 with the knowledge

that not to resist

       means being swept away.

      You are manipulating me.

After the wind has found no pleasure here,

            the scabby tree prevails,

apples clear upon the empty branches.

No answer have I for these brandings, these lightbulb filaments, these excruciaments.

I find myself

    returning

        to the succulent corpses in the naked tree,

curious, baffled,

     without will or explanation,

          trying to turn them off.

These Are The Fine Days Of My Ordinary Life

Good poems open holes in our heads. Good Holes.
Good bullets too. Yes, I'm fine.

The unknown soldier sprays half his face and falls, limbs
        released into a thin sort of beauty, the kind Picasso
    tried to get rid of in his ugly, child art.

I can fit all my knuckles in my mouth and this does not hurt.
And would one know, after my last breath, that calm water was just above
                my lips?

My walls where headlights veer at corners are smeared with Sammy's pictures.
I can watch her for hours just as I can place my hand over a candle.

In its cabinet, its brown bottle, how peaceful the imovane.
And in their closet, her clothes. I wash and fold each week.

And wake at all hours in different corners of my rooms. I'm fine.
She may return.

I do not fear the Sitka spruce lined up like minds pushed to the side.
I can go where strawberries go, to a place where they cannot bear even
gentleness.

And it is warm there. And comforting:
I tell myself when I am well I won't love you anymore.

What The Walls Say

"There's something wrong with you," at the top of the landing, she said, "I could always tell," sideways at my picture. "See?" A small explosion of mouth liquid in the hairs of my face. That woman, firmly planted feet, only in panti-hose and spread on stuff, could take a blackhead between her fingernails and squirt it on the mirror, lean over just so for hours combing the scabs on her face then turn to me still at my photograph by the high, round window like a dove with a crushed-in chest. "You've made my face look awful."

Her, being that woman whose body fits you better than any other?

Well ... yes. Then beyond the landing, barricaded myself in the spare bed-room while she screamed at the other side of the door. "You are abusing me. You bastard." How slow the hour hand sweeped the nights I sat in a chair and with the sun got up again and another time raised the kids. Now I have a life and a declining bank balance. It breaks out on my skin who panics without alprazolam. You can hardly believe somedays the walls speak to me.

Really? What do they say? These walls of yours.

Lying on the couch in the afternoon, eye tricking one and another way, nerves coming out of the roof and the other, veins set in to it, shadows, I think, how the mind works. How a mind apprehends pomegranites and utters the opposite. How the mind steps one small thought and another until it is something else again.

What possibly can you mean, my friend?

Do you understand I feel so crazy at first. I hear nothing, then in all those unopposable corners I remember ...

that she laid money at the feet of your daughters, that her tactics prove your inno-cence, that she said nothing other than yes to everyone other than you, that she rode horses over you like a tide, that you couldn't fold clothes correctly, that you played and she was a real person, that she said black but you, childishly, insisted white, that everyone agreed with her, that her grip came at you like an ostrich face...

All I thought I was wrong.

And you did it for the best, didn't you? Close the door on that part of your life? And wasn't it so hard, at home eight years, and don't you feel so guilty for hurting your children, because you were there for them and you'd have to be inhuman to leave your children because closing that door was like killing them? Wasn't it? And she said she only begged you for them and didn't you have no commitment because you only waited twenty years? All she ever wanted you to do was become another person because she always knew there was something wrong with you.

... things i don't know im thinking ...

i can talk to people i am okay then i wake and then i wake and it is the same black night in the same clothes i wore yesterday i work an hour and lie on my bed and vibrate lie under the blanket leave a sweat body on the sheet i go out on the bent over streets i can go to the school to meet the kids and say hello to people far away and above me i see myself take an axe and hit them across the head see their skulls split open and i hit my head to stop seeing the severed heads of my daughters i am ok a bottle of wine in a glass a small glass and another and then alprazolam i change from the sound a cat makes when i step on it now i see daylight falling over the trees the walls moving by dewdrops splintering the grass i have friends i do not talk to i eat and grow thin sleep and have no dreams the ceiling of my room goes white to black to white to bed and bookshelf something i can hold onto photographs of sammy all over the livingroom beds like cemeteries thin vanessas climb the walls i throw up and nothing comes out im paralyzed at the computer and nothing comes out i love this woman i cant say and she will come and live with me she does not love her husband she will come to me and everything will be all right she wants me but i cant speak to her everything will be all right she will bring her daughter and it will be all right she approves of me like my father i am poor but he is not dying i discover my days standing at the calender i have not eaten feel my ribs feel the skin over my stomach dreading the bank statement dreading slipping my finger under the edge dreading the rip of paper the figures sliding down i am full of control but it is never anywhere two times i have sat on the doorstep watching the cherry blossoms fall bloom and fall and freeze and bloom im okay i have my own life but nobody im so alone in here way in here and no one ever comes i stop the ringing in my ears with acetominophen on nights when my knees ache i force myself to eat but take no pleasure its okay i dont have a job that woman has stolen my children mucous coming down my face i put my eyes on the concrete so no one will notice me my head is the sound a cat makes when i step on it but it stops for a few hours with imovane bitter blue pills i slip away then light transforms darkness into bed and bookshelf havent i done this before oh im so tired of talking to myself dennis i am making my own life in my own house the bank owns most of im not worried i might turn religious ive taken my pills lorazepam is just fine i totally and unconditionally love and accept myself just the way i am all i want is a cigarette thats all just one if hell give me just one i asked a month ago i go to the service station i can feel him thinking he doesnt like me so i buy a paper and ask and i buy a coke and ask i buy some milk and ask he is walking away from me in his black and orange and grey crisp jacket i can feel my mind going i can feel the feeling of a battery on my tongue i am okay the pills dont work but i take more i put my fingernails in my arms yes im here yes i hold on

New Brain

I recall horses shouldering through their own breath, and then the winter.
A trodden hillside. Pale birch trunks, their dark scars. And then they were the trees.

How can you hate such beauty?

Well, Northern lights with the quality of tall music over miles of abandoned snow.
Leading them home, I fall among the reins and swing
        in the leathers as hooves walk through my chest.

An accident. Surely.

Then the spring I stood my ground in lightning. Rain the size of plums.
The polo pony part of the fence and me scared shitless with my chainsaw
        in the zang of breaking wire. The smoke of me cutting him free.

Yes, but how can you hate them?

I think you have no ears for me. Hear the quarter horse with a summer stump
through his ribs, irises crazed as blue liver flowers, the puddingness of his blood.
For me, horses go on this way: la malaise des cheveux.

*Dennis, Dennis, in the lowlands of the estuary, they're harvesting cauliflower like new
brains, the slice of the kirpal knife, the white prize held to that high October light.*

Take away my brain in autumn? But first tell me how any hatred can be rational.

Tell Me What I Hear Through A Telescope The Wrong Way

Here I open my eyes on the day you do not come home.
Now it is winter, and my washed hand smokes in the winter air.

This would be the place obligation and desire have no quarrel,
the calm of a leathery sea. 16 years after you crossed over
    into this world.

       The curtain flutters as though dropped
    through the fingers of someone not there, Elvis Presly perhaps,
  with those spaghetti legs and gold trousers, unquellable nigger legs

on a white boy, his never-again drips of hair another era away.
        A stylus skips in an unimportant
   corner of my thoughts:

here I convince myself of hope - crazy, and complete, and all:

   I think I hear my daughter   take my heart
      with a smoking hand.

Avoiding Four Leaf Clovers

Here a better moon rises and the lawn fills with blades too small to see.
My life grows slender, you see, emptied of my daughter, her one barefoot
       softly in front of the other.

"I just don't like your house. Don't want to move."
Said with intent not to wound, and in the present tense.
"Don't want my friends to see me like this."

Here, and only for me, the moon leads to a better place:
where the Spanish loaded cattle those centuries ago,
where English ladies picked four leaves.

"I'm closer to my horse. Why can't you understand?"
But that is why I am here, and the price I pay is you.

"I'll phone. I will," she says and six months slip into another place.
Where seagulls sink out of the sky,
I pick petals at Clover Point: I love you, no I don't ...

weeping will bring no other end;
her mother will buy a white car and wash away the tears,
Sammy's brown eyes more like mine than anyone's.

All of her is a wish to be loved. Do you know an endless wish?
It is like a cancer. Someone will do her in with herself.

Blown open by moonlight, I understand there are times
we live only part of our lives. And this may be necessary.

I take a premonition into a future that includes me no more.
There I wait with one hand over the other.

This is when the insects come, columns of them
in the late flat sun. The sound their wings make

beating holes in the air; listening to myself;
the part that goes on inspite of everything.

Why do I crouch and crouch here, sore to the bone?

'Sur le pont d'Avignon, on y danse, on y danse'

That former wife might die. It might be wished for her, incandescent and true
as a nail driven through an X-ray,

as that daylight marking blitzkrieg from the others,
tarmac liquifying to shoes and then their people,

frizzling where they stood,
hair like torches in some lower circle of hell.

Less explicit hatreds are possible:
                    the silent disease of understanding, say,
          or guilt that never gets to regret.

In my own life, a longing survives:
arm in arm with Samantha,
                    the haphazard ambience of game;
                         warm, huge flakes of snow
                    folding across her cheeks. And the smell of cinnamon.
The sound of laughing children in the winter air.

But truly there is only
a backyard of blue snow, shadows that sweep across the land of their own accord.

I wish and turn away. As we do from insects
burning on a log in the grate.
                    Oh, yes, I care, my friend, but it doesn't reach me.

Afterwards, The Amputated Arm Tells The Mind It's Still There

I do not mean to say I brood about children as they recede.
I go with them. I stay here. That is what I mean.

How long am I?
Well, where does a father get to, declaring
accept me for who I am, where I am?
And then she answers,

and be my daddy too.

Now I will tell you how long I am.
Longer than I am.

Occipital, Parietal, Sphenoid, Frontal, Temporal, Ethmoid

Rain when it touches the face like the ends of swimming hair.
        I do not easily forget such precision; how naturally
                the eight bones of her skull came apart, how they flowed

through her mother's hips which had previously known only the love we rode
one another to.
             "You have your retirement for hobbies," her mother called, and
called my name from her naked body on the stairs.
         In the flooded basement of the duplex Richardson I listened
at my electric trypewriter and went insane.

Adjusting that October night to redefine the decisive moment
        I put my hand under her warm, wet, five-minute head, terrified.
Memory insists the room was white, or maybe green.
The room where I smoked and passed out. Winter fire flared across the wall
      like a kind of intelligence. I could not understand anything

as blurred as the future,
               the passionless efficiency with which a birthday candle
would one day set fire to her hair.

The way an orchid becomes part of a tree, I carried my daughter those years.
The days I ran with her down the long hall and circled the fireplace in a room
        that smelled of fish.
Her mother brought home her breasts, milk letting down through her brown silk
blouse.

The news detatched itself from its paper and rose up the chimney.
"If you loved me, you wouldn't write that poetry anymore."

Years distant. The far and peaceful end of a Sunday.
In the untamed street the wind-chime now peeling,

                              the afternoon paper
wrapping late spring peonies, a dripping

                         of petals on the unwashed stairs of the other
     house.
This has all been true and passing time makes it no different.

                              Tell me what a father is.
Tell me to let go: the exact way a Siamese fighting fish will turn and rip its own image
to pieces.

IF WHERE WE LIVE AN EMPIRE OF LONGING WHAT THEN
                              –Erin Mouré

... where you first live a pile of twisted bedclothes and a lime-coloured crib.
                    Behind bars your face floating.

Now we discover myth way out here on a beach that is seldom in. Stepping on
                    sanddollars. The crack of their limestone backs and our calling it
                              good luck.

Now you run a race on a crooked grass track and tell me you almost won.
                    I see your brown eyes and no one back there.

Now you are fourteen and glamourous, remote as sunglasses, in a swimming pool
                    your grandfather built for you. Your eyes slide away from me.

Now the mark your warm foot leaves for awhile on Spanish tile. Me
                    the patience of clouds turning themselves inside out...

O derange!
These end years I live alone in green suede slippers, as a life lived toward the end of a
        poem
                    in a house where the wreckage of summer rises in a white line.

        Yet I am said to be safe in all my whiteness, and shouldn't I be happy,
                    behind my brass locks?

        Who says this? *Why, toujours la même chose: everyone.*

What Happens When We Tend Animals More Intelligent Than Ourselves

Geese, in lifting from the paddock, turn from black to white on white and disappear.
The in a room sound of hooves across a wooden bridge.

And it goes on like this, putting hands into gloves, giving orders
to the neck of a horse, the scent of hogfuel, confusion.
        The raisined scent of pee.

I cannot comprehend the wiring of finger on neck.
        But to see the animal move under a girl who is also mine.

Piaffe, passage, half pass, those imperceptible fingers
        make the horse round and turn. Braid my hair
            I might gush and rise to the height of an animal.

            *

Afternoon at that exact moment when light comes out of things.
Breeched and sixteen, she reaches through the distance and takes my arm.

        "Je t'aime you, Daddyo."

O, how that light can make me foolish.
The quality of light in that country, Pasture 4: me and my teenager,
        a bathtub full of whirligigs.

        Je t'aime you too.

Saying Goodbye To Pain

- for Patrick and Deborah

The last poem opens to departure, a train station I have never been to, and steam
        upon the window,
                the sound of a straw broom
over broken pavement.
           The phone call I received unexpectedly,
                       and early,
asking for a ticket away.
          Little brown eyes. I could have called her this,
sung her this song:
        how we love the heart when it breaks in us;
                      how longing
chains us to the moment it takes over,
              landscape blurring outside the window.
The whistle moves through itself,
       a voice that feels its clearing,
             a record on which a finger is pushed.
There is a certain amount of time
         as the station is relinquished.
                The time it takes
to reach the point steadily,
        crossing whatever land there is.
How hard the wooden bench,
        this deuxieme classe, how unattainable but necessary
her destination.
       Rubbing a square window in an arc of wave,
              the child is safe
from the knowledge
       that life falls away from itself.
                 Not to speak
in the brown-eyed world
       would be to reach not resolution,
             bread,
                 "Goodbye."

Designing The Perfect Woman

...we've been around, we fall, we fly
we mostly fall, we mostly run
and every now and then we try
to mend the damage that we've done

                                              –LC

Being True

I am a door
that opens and opens.

I am a bird, flying
to your forbidden body.

I am delicious, fragile,
an invalid in summer.

Lie on my pillow.
There are no keys for my heart.
You know this.

Do not let me sleep.
I would be someone else.

Touch me here and here.
When I stop hurting

I'll still want you.
I will not forget

how the palm unfolds a garden,
that joy is a simple fruit.

Lift me
with your summer fingers.

Petals are falling even now.
I am lost and I do not care.

I want.

The Longing

Zeus chopped humans in half. For this reason,
love is a longing to be whole through finding
one's other half.

- after Aristophanes

Is there only one?
The half that is blood and leaks away.

The half that is hair into which I sink.
The half that is patternless crockery, bed sheets
and crumpled clothes,

the stain that is love,
the tangled limbs that are an instance of love.

There is the half that is economy, goose bumps,
that requests the necessary gold, that makes a kitchen new,
apron strung over morning breasts.

The half that is scars a finger may trace for decades
and not find the end unless
the scarred one steps out of them.

The half in love with a violin,
the swell of its brown thigh.

The half that is a wall of leather books,
a mind like a conductor's baton

that roves the various cells and makes them play.
The sensual mind coming apart at the seams

with skin turned into summer, white eyes,
the slice a shoulder makes in blue water.

The half that is a hand when the other
searches without eyes for what is missing
and names it desire.

How a hand changes to fit around fingers.

How a hand grows liver spots that sprawl across another
needy of its strength;
this is also a food that for today is enough.

And what about the half I truly want, the she
who completes my sentences? Perhaps she doesn't live.

Half of me is shy, and my love is at first sight
and hidden, not expressed:

the half that is synapse, endorphic,
domestic as a cheerio, exotic

as the woman who has not been told
I'd like her to be mine.

Her lips reveal many people.
My love sits on a twig.

Then there is the rejected half, the discovery
of longing as a knife. That half turns away.

A seagull slips across the window:
longing after my other half

and, of course, the plaguing question:
is there only one?

Love Songs And Negotiations

I could tell you I love you.
I could walk off a cliff.

I could look in the mirror
and see you.

Why torment me
you other man's wife,

who more than fills my head?
How can I negotiate

when my heart is
no longer my own?

This then is a love song.
A day for iguanas

whose pale shadows
etch the long rocks.

Sure your happiness pleases me.
Your radar glows in my limbs

and yes

there are the mundane icebergs
of my life: divorce, no job,

two children.
The place where hands meet

is tomorrow.
The place I will tell you

is a mountain.
You are so beautiful in this turvy field,

blonding in rods of sun,

hear me
now I am speechless:

twin.

the warm

the pool of warm a body makes
the flare of your hip

the small depression
that fits my hand
in the dark

rolling thunder
takes hold of you
and then it lets you go

the body
is simple as rain
simple as the day
and just as ancient

there is no night

i am a candle
on the far side of pain

reach a long eye
close your arms

shh
you be a secret

i will keep you

Designing The Perfect Woman

Waltz with me these decades,
nylon-toed on the hardwood floor.

Talk to me of everything.
I hear only your red-rinsed hair
on my shoulder.

Tomorrow you'll be blonde
and I'll be dumbfounded.
Pray for me

in your black leather jacket,
your hint of skirt.

Desire is a tuning fork.
Respect is the angel of the soul.
Your wings I fall and fall into.

I turn to the unspeakable
beauty of a brassiere
unfurling its mastectomized breast.

You blonde-eyed lover of lobelia
with greying pubic hair.

Life descends fifty basis
points and you are radiant
in a blazer and string of pearls.

Love is the lace in old-people's eyes.
Share the finite drink called life.
How far we travel to quench a thirst,

woman I walk beside
and only then, lean on.

Love At Yellow Point Lodge

They are why we sleep
and why upon waking, bewildered by the day
the white lions rise with us in the sun
and move with great patience toward the mind.
                                    Patrick Lane

They are why we sleep
these August days, drowning, swift and deep.
Truth is all provisional, happiness
is in the viscera, something to keep
the gift of screws and more worthy than gold.
The beautiful endures,
this tawny fur, rangy in my hand.
How to scratch the ear of a lion
unflinching at its rumbled pleasure?
I eat peaches insatiably

and why upon waking, bewildered by the day,
do I remember a hand ripped off in a casual way?
A hand may hold an arm, feel out
the bifurcate furrows of sandstone that lay
sweltering in the sun's love. Here you come
slendering the sandstone in lemon stockings
that go all the way to here,
lady who never photographs twice the same,
whose body is a magnet, whose mind is irresistible.
Here I am, hands in pockets in love, and now

the white lions rise with us in the sun,
chessmen advancing the sandstone run.
I no longer desire protection thick enough for pain.
The world we left strips like skin.
We know the bed we will share this first time
away from families, in a breathless world.
Decisions have a bitterness we taste
to be who we are: the rasp of a feline tongue
rips off skin and brings forth sweetness.
Hold me like a peach

and move with great patience toward the mind.
Walking our mountain of years we might find
the sea in all its sluicing goes where it goes,
you with slippers in your hand.
What I know is this:
when burned I spread on ointment
and walk around the fire.
White lions walk with me, waist high, Victorian,
a tree the shape of lightning, and you
lady in lemon stockings that go all the way to here.

The Seductive Curve Of Darkness
In The Viola's *F* Hole

In seventeen twenty seven,
Stradivarius ran his eye down a
long smooth thigh, with his chisel and
his sandpaper and his incessant wood hammer
wooed music from a block of wood that a man stands
within his black and white tailed suit and coaxes the essence
he practiced the many decades. Above him his audience, in wigs
and gowns and ribbons, swirls of cherubes climbing the walls. He touches
his long white bow, the horse hair strand to the fine gut string and the viola begins
to tremble in front of thousands of people who've paid dearly for this exposal. He draws
his bow and there comes a gasp, and tears from their eyes, for the music pouring from the
rich brown wood is the ache for nimble fingers.

                         Inside the brown viola is a woman, reclining
on a pillow. Her hands rest as though in prayer in her nylon lap. Her bare shoulder leans
against blue-flowered walls and her eyes are closing. Her neck arches as she
listens to the music welling-up in her body. The strap slips from her bare
brown shoulder, down her bare brown arm, exposing the swell
of her breast, tinged with sun from her tiny curved windows.
Now the aureole emerges, now the nipple, coming
together in a tiny o. And the strap is slipping
lower, falling with her hair. Almost on its own
her hand unfurls, reaches in to stroke
her clitoris, and play the world's
oldest music.

The Danger Of Loving Someone Not Here

What will be is not; and what would be;
what was, what might have been,
they are not.
—Paul Valery

I think of my father who one day threw a telephone through a window and kept me
                     in a state of terrification, saying won't you please approve of me.

Not so strange I loved you before I met you, squinting,
          boney-kneed, up the driveway, anorexia a kind word for your demons.

His father had laid his small body on the black and white linoleum and beat him
with a belt to make him stand.

The children of Lir were changed to swans. A millennium they fought back through snow
              and withering ice to the end: plucked free of feathers
and murdered. Heaven was gained for their souls but nothing that they wanted:
                   the warmth of a long dead father.

JFK took off to the moon in a streak of brain. Jackie sat in her coral dress, splattered as
she was in him, and negotiated another man of charm and ethnicity, only just removed
from the old round table.

You said you would live, "In another place, another time."
And shrugged your prettyness, this woman that you are, tasting menopause, the purple
          of a better century.

                          Little wonder all I could do was shake
from wanting you
        to get away. After years of shrink I learned that pain is a burden we pick up and
carry.
We have to learn to let it go.

So damn your yellow ribbons and damn your Alligheri signature, all that beautiful
consuming
fire. Damn your Mary Queen of Scotts in her pointy little shoes.
All your winning which signifies

56

nothing but the prevailing colour of Hell.

Saanich Inlet invades with sweet persuasion.
Geraniums splash the plaster walls of a mansion that bears my fathers name.

                                  To see his Parkinson-trembly hands, the feet
that cannot feel the ground, is to perceive a quiet measure of love that ought not be denied.
I can put my finger through the Tiger Moth he flew across a Canada younger
                        than the aged, murdered children. Returned from all his voyages,
                              came a gentle boy.

Coupling is a lesser measure of intimacy and not the request of mine. I love you
     as a daughter and ask you, please come back.

Because you are so beautiful, because you are my father, because I fall away from all my
resolve, because . . . . because I care.

Perhaps The First Love Poem

No great feat to flick a switch. A lifted finger and the sudden, ambery porch materializes the lesser beings.

In the afterness of sex, I willingly release a sigh. Deborah charts a shirt to a gauzy pattern. Her lips aboriginal, untamable as summer. Pins she plucks from a plush red strawberry.

Maybe Eve didn't like her fruit, a ripe brown fig like a misplaced scrotum in the licheny branches of an apple tree. Maybe the snake

had a hard time convincing her to put it in her mouth, and she, no dummy, had Adam taste a part of himself he never before could reach.

So perhaps it is fruit in my simple hand, perhaps it is pain. I smell sweet seedy genitals across a thin skin of centuries - the thirty five chemicals it takes to plumpen up an apple!

Or say in my evening chair, about to turn the light like some indulgent immanence, I will recall the delicate toes of elk stepping among the remnant snows indifferent
as beauty is to itself;

or, Napoleon in his foolish suede boots retreating from January. The mane of his horse. The way it casually fractured the air.

Every bit as doomed as the soft-winged insects flying resolutely out of nothing. I can do no more than point and say, there goes something dead. Then the smoke lifts
from ruined lives.

Deborah has spent her whole life walking toward this orange home. She holds herself among the moving crates, the dried bananas like shrunken heads along the counter. Simple: the meaningless desires with which we fill up our days. And night?
Too much of everything.

Which returns me to the pulpy early nectarines, to the question of sex and love, the secret language of our isolated beds of now. The dusky peaks of her pelvic crowns my hand can reach across.

I hold Deb out like a bolt of living cloth, two wrists bound by my right hand,
two ankles in my left, and marvel at the rounded female generosity of her flowered
blue panties, intuition, where we join in gift.

Which leads me to God. The Bible was written by layers and layers of men who first held
up their religion to the scrutiny of themselves, their belief in the very sexual
mushroom.

And there is a certain amount of horror, as I grow nimble and fleet of foot,
to rephrase the older poet, and shoulder down His long straight road.

And if longing is being stuck, what then of ambivalence?

What then if God was one of us?

What It Means To Be Human

Where my masculinity coincides with humanity
stands australopithecus in a suit and tie

raising his club
over a ditch of skeletons in Cambodia.

The answer is the seductive curve
of darkness in a viola's *f* hole,

a baby rasping a breast
in African night, small tongue
barely scraping the world.

It is an eye, a river
that starts nowhere and goes nowhere
but the flowing matters.

It is sitting by the dusty road
as hawks fill the air,

the Kuban, pogroms, peasants in orange scarves,
broad gritty fingernails
fretting the shrinking Aral Sea.

It is Ghaddafia, swirling
in masquerades of leadership, oil that surges
beneath his feet,

the rattling of sabres, penises blasting into space.
It is warfare and tractor beams,
lights that flash in the night,

cruise missiles
that have flown too long.
It is rivers of commerce,

vats of human indigo bugs in India

60

sweating for Calvin Klein jeans.
It is prayer wheels and ragged lace,
the Dalai Lama, forgetting

this poem line after line because it's too long, too assaulting.
It is the scarab beetle,
the ground-in fear of snakes,

faith that is a sunrise,
the small congregation
clapping hands in a Venezuelan night,
smoke of their fires drifting up.

It is penguins swimming through sleeping children.

It is when I bend myself straight
to correct the glittering iconoclasm
of poetry that does not make me happy

yet fills me with brilliance and a kind of comfort.
It is the things we do not understand
and believe just the same,

the cinticlian rituals,
sway of hips and incense,
thinking both ways.

Compassion walks like a cloud,
and firelight, the serene lonely desert
hollow out the insides,

leave us strength like a hunger.
It is the twisted forms of life,
the Hitlers, Stalins, Pol Pots, Idi Amins,
the massacre of dignity that demands
us to be vigilant,

of the need for collective good will,

jobs that work,
the rule of law and spill of water.
It is these indelible images

that will never stop ripping from my mind,
the greater things than what I want,
choosing people over defending territory.

It is being furious for the broken woman
broken by the broken man
but somewhere the blame must be cast,

somewhere the courage must be found
to say *mea culpa*
and reach from the eroding will.

We are small and limited,
far away from the rest of us
and we raise our crude religions against the dark,

because that is what we do,
because we are human.

The rough wooden tray of skulls
held aloft by australopithecus
is a Cambodian ossuary.

That one white skull to the side
is not huge, the others are small and

the realization, the outrage, the unending howl,
is humanity where it's at:

loose ends and resonance, mahagony.

Love And Other Things That Hurt

...tonight, tonight I cannot rest
I've got this joy here inside my breast
to think that I did not forget
that child, that song of Bernadette

–LC

The Girl From The Far Country

I am lost and I do not care; poetry
fills me with brilliance and a kind of comfort.

—anon

Exile is a country she never knew
was actually hers,

a surprise, a kind of freedom,
from everything but herself.

Self posession is a stiff drink, a mirror;
the two of her are strong and young and beautiful.

Her mind moves within its brain
in a way her face cannot comprehend.

Back from the other she stares at her,
at the people behind her eyes.

How she longs for all her skin,
for the fruit that would kiss her out.

The god upon her is her father's.
Her nipples for His blue blue eyes.

And her fingers keep on coming,
smoothing the holy surfaces

There she stands insatiable:
blue jeans and denim shirt, girlish pumps.

How warm with salt her arm
under a suddenly blue sun.

The courtyard fills with horses, ordained cloth;
does she fear she is invisible?
Does she fear she'll die too soon?
The eye that is upon her is mostly her own.

—anon

She would lower her hand like Joan of Arc,
believes she would give freely

of her milk to more than her own child,
her mind's little girl in a party dress,
oh so pretty,

the splash of blue and red flowers,
the floppy straw hat.

Her eyelids are halfway open, halfway full,
with a full-grown tongue tasting a turned corner.

How far away this girl, how close the woman inside,
gravid with her abilities,

timid at the old inn door.

She knows the body you punish is your own,
the one you also pleasure.

Now I will tell you about the voices.
I do not hear them, I speak them.
I speak before I hear.
I do not know what I say, but I am healed
                              –Frederyk Chopin

There are times when the air rips open
to reveal the rest of her life,

tangible as bread,
the long and varigated road,

oiled with sun. Pain is a gecko pinned
with toenails to its white-washed plaster wall.

The voices in her head imagine Greece, an Abbey of Versimilitude,
a terracotta plateia, Anthony Quinn grizzled,

all the old movie stars crooning about the war,
drinking drinks with swizzle sticks,

dreaming about San Francisco,
and the glorious

fifties that made them famous.
Elizabeth Taylor smoothes her latest

facelift, and there's the leaching blue of
Sinatra's eyes. Dean Martin, Danny Kaye.

She is a snapped stick with all she understands:
the urge to scream out of her skin

and make contact, that touching is holy,
as is opening eyes, the good intention performed.

That wind is a door, as is sunrise,
holding the neck of a battered person,
interpreting his will,

allowing herself to be hurt
and knowing when to say no more.

It is not for her voices to say what she must do:

the doors in her body are closed with needles
shoved through her flesh.

Yet, they suggest trust,
that the injury has been salved too long
by winning the yellow ribbons.
Perhaps, they say, the little girl
remains in her flowery dress

until they are discarded.
The fear that fuels her excellence?

That of being ordinary, unchosen.
She understands there are no Platonic forms,

but does not feel it,
that creation is in her heart.

How very strange, as that is where she lives.

She adopts the voices of other human beings,
all her movie stars and churchmen,

all her men in soiled trousers,
to be herself,

to be enough.
This is also her gift, they tell her,

so a delicate exorcism for her muse.
'Release,' she hears but does not speak,
'release the little girl in yellow underpants.'

The door of my brain opens to the wild grace
of belonging in this field more than in myself

—anon

She would shake her long hair wet,
fringe the hills with rain

before she returns to her own country.
And she would walk miles into the hills
and she would follow the sure man this once
and she would sit, bare feet tucked under her
before the amphitheatre of Greece
under a once-again blue sun.

This girl from the far country
with vaguely oriental eyes,
half-closed with hormonal tide,

her unblemished body,
she endlessly feels surrounded by.

How she desires and disregards
the admiration of men.

How she would be annointed.
There is a door and it swings one way,

and she must go when it calls
and she must go through

or stay in the room of being young,
stay less than she was meant to be.

The draughty Agean is semolina
pushed and pushed.

Her brain opens like a tangerine.
How bitter and bleak your tongue,
how jealous if you cannot taste her.
Taste her.

In the cathedral of the heart
reside the seeds of all you are.
They reach, they burn, they grow.

                                        —anon

There is also a man,
with a staff of blue and red and gold.

There is an olive tree, shimmering without wind,
leaves turning silver.

Its fruit is from the rainbow,
its apples and oranges,
its lemons succulent as the sun.

His mind is a slow arrow.
Black pants he wears, black vest.

Oil from his plate, he wipes
through his hair.

Four peaks for his britches in his trouser waist,
a thick brown belt besides.

And the girl turns a circle
as that father in her mind
in that other world of hers

is single-stroking 2 by 4s
into the great blue beyond,

St. Christopher covered in sweat.
"I know who you are," says he.

"How is this possible?" Her eyes reside
on cherries so gaspably red,

on red-fleshed strawberries so bruisable,
fingers rise in her eyes.

He answers and he answers,
"I just know. They grow. No mystery, girl."

For now the headman - one step forward shoots
...to strike the absolute centre of my skull
my absolute centre somehow
with such skill
such staggering lightness
that the blow is love.

- P.K. Page

She has journeyed around the world -
though she did not know -

to be melted by Aganippe water.
Oh those lucky, lucky days

when the air rips open, the blue sky
reveals truth at every door,

the jagging of the reticular system,
the very god who once melted faces off the earth.

Elbows to her frangible ribs,
she knows the thread is ripping;
the hags are cutting her father free.

She wears her love like a see-through dress,
galaxy spattered, sequins drawn from the night.

And the sure man
who with his shepherd's staff lead her into
these hills that have no colour

lifts the big dipper on its stick
and begins to pour

into her frightened, sleeping mind.
He scoops out her brain, licks its sweet folds,

washes and washes it
to a bright shy cauliflower.

The dippers of Aganippe pour down
all the days of her life.

Merciless lord, she's talking in tongues.
She rises, and she rises whitely.

Love And Other Things That Hurt

1. I'm Speaking To You Small As The President

"I am speaking to you,"
he says as he lies among his blood

in the soft strings of rain.
"Bowlegged ladies wrestle
cellos for my music, military and festive."

Oh, men, she thinks and sighs a draughty
century. Oh their great swords
that fall big as pins.

"Hey, girlie, I'm speaking to you.
My wounds are lips that speak my praise."

She swings her flamenco dress and stamps
her slim heels, eyes him like a queen.

Pupils at the bottoms of his eyes, he rebegins,

"I am asking with hands of oil and unstrangled doves.
I am asking in Jerusalem.
I am asking at the end of the last road

of my life for any old conflagration."

He fidgets into a heap of wrung hands,
dents himself with chains.
He would stand with two legs spread for her, walk on water ...

and she?

She thinks he'll be tender as glue until desire disappears.
She hears the crop go smack.
Sees banners of blood leap across the cell,

the electric cord, snapping in the groin.

"I am clutching blind eyes on a mountain top, woman.
The world doesn't care.

Let me kiss you through the bars of my face.
Let the hugest building rise like a brontosaurus
in my head.

I am asking in your cathedral.
I am asking from my ventricals.
I am asking with need turned inside out

for any old crumb of war."

*

Of course her heart is a weed jerked by the sea,
and her eyes are gathered from many women,
and her nostrils keen the air
for something she cannot smell.
And her breasts are a wave
and her legs are long, run dark through the sun.

And of course there is a melting of Antarctic in the Sahara,
and she is warmth in a lost forest.
How she despises weakness and falls for this man.

"Do you kiss with your eyes open," says he.
"Do you love a dead man's friend?"

"Don't I love you?" Eyes closed, she kisses him
inside

the place a kiss explodes and no one cares why.

And her arms melt to his limbs.
And her legs take him in.

Her dress presents thigh and unguarded pubis,
the world that opens its eye,

the lips that are her wound.
She drowns him in her body.

In the instant lightning strikes
he views his architecture on his eyelids,

the immense dignity of lions moving toward
the presidency. The machete, the razor.
The bars of black and white policy.

Then he's soft as plasticine.
She is helplessly complete,
a circle slipping down the air.

He fires a bazooka through his head,
and still he sees her.

Trust me, trust me, she might cry,
in a voice that means no harm.

Instead, "Husha, husha," and closes his eyes.
"It's only the sound of your gun."

2. Religion, The Heart In Its Firmament

These doors once touched yield like flesh,

and from walking between the rain,
he is a mind that won't stop coming.

Admiring his gowns, he admires himself.
Shouldering the air aside, he speculates:
a cathedral is a place in the bone,

so far from bone
it's love blowing through us.

He feels nothing but his surplice and stole,
his starched white petticoats,
women's lingerie all over his flesh.

"Don't touch me, I'm filled with the Lord."
In his eyes she flits like deelie boppers,
approximately Tinker Bell,
diminutive and sweet, harmless as a sparrow.

"But there are bills to be paid," she frustrates
two inches from his powdered nose.

"I can swing the holy clippers.
I can recite the Vedic Recipes.
I can avoid the holes in your skin."

He feels the peace of rules.
He would marry his sisters on the advice of sentences.
He would bow to the east, the west regular as grammar.

Next she is nailed by his grandness to granite pillars.
Kissable ankles and 13 ribs. Her breasts hang bereft
and lovely.
Her fingers dig grooves in the rock.

Is this the way to God? she might implore if this
were the way to dignity.

She knows religion is a subtle instinct heavy as chain,
a voluntary frontal lobotomy.

"I love the smell of black leather
books in the morning. Smells like scruples."

And the sphere's keep on singing,
the heavens keep on falling into his pocket.
Angels keep dancing on pins.

"I can make you real."
To his high stone ceilings, God smears like perfume.
In his mind she is a candle, meekly upbended,
her long giraffe neck exposed.
His love is a light switch. It can't be sort of on.

"I would instruct you on the ways of your people.
And I would hand you
the ribbons of usuality, and the hammer
you make bread with and the saw you make fire,
and the drill you make sound,
the red fluid that eats holes in reality.
I would instruct you and I would give freely,
on the days of your passage,
on the veils you must wear,
on the iron fist in the velvet glove,
the freedom of chains."

She feels her feet in a dance not of her own making
and she feels years drain from her face,
and she sees her hands wring teatowels
for no particularly terrible reason.

But her voice

is a sea that has ended its travelling,
a wind gone perfect, a seed
so beautiful it need not bloom.

She shrugs off the drowning,
the dreams of living forever after she's dead,
and shakes her head resolutely,
for she has no answer other than he's wrong.

Other than he has no ears for truth,
in all his truth. No word for heart
in its firmament.

The longest journey is between his ears
and he can't get there from where he's at

lounging on a cloud in need of rescue,
stretching a finger *for her.*

Ecstacy is a pale and flimsy thing,
she thinks, and then rethinks.

Haven't I thinked this before,
turned in this younger light

getting younger, the terrible backward sound
of the universe shrinking into the snout
of its own big bang?

She is a shred of de ja vu, but not afraid.
He spits out a bland wafer, sees himself smallen
in her eye. "I have values, I have worth..."

Yes and yes.
She silences his fears with a small hand
that rubbers high into his universe.

Ermine robes slip from his limbs and he is a man sore afraid.

How weird his lingerie.

He sees the hard-edged world, it's eagerness to bruise,
and covers his eyes.

It comes to pass that she holds his hand on the ground
in the blinding light.

Close your eyes and see
me.

You are a door. A soft warm door.

3. Tribal Man And The Threads Of The Social Contract

And so it shall always come to pass
that the blind man
comes to terms with the dirt in his hands.

Anemones open and close in her eyes
as he picks up any old yoke and lays it on his

collarbones.
Though the earth refuses to tilt
and the sky is unimpressed

with a burden sinking
huge as a buffalo into bone,

he is Quasimodo,
rappelled from his apple tree.
"How lucky to be ordinary,
a worm down the throat of the early bird."

Dust is a yellow dog
and the earth accepts his sweat.

Trudging his life is tracing fingerprints
in smaller and smaller circles.
The earth falls open like hands after prayer.

"Hold me," she says and her flesh is a pendulum
he would wade through rock to bend.
They burn mushrooms in frizzling nights,
erect warm empires with firelit bodies.

On the ninth month her pelvis cracks.
Chldren appear from a thicket
in a downpour of blood.

There is organ music from the trees and the insistent bird.

His legs are streams of liver,
"Am I still here?"

"For the first time."

It is now he understands the divine
smell of a baby's forehead.
His days rise and fall like green.
The landscape goes with him.

And still her vulva rips.
Children tiptoe the corners of his field,
mass among his furrows.

Behind his eyes, they change the world;
his brain becomes a heart; death becomes impossible.
The sun is a dove with many arms.

                              *

When he has dragged the last stoneboat free
and when he has cast the stones,
when bullrush smoke drifts like a smile
and the eye is finally white,
there might be peace.

When the rubbers are stacked heel to toe,
when the underpants are folded,
when the ear hears footsteps on paths not yet taken,
it might be evening.

The children have leapt into tall
and found it fits like their own perfect futures.

Daughters in frocks become what wolves desire.
Sons finger his deformity and shake their heads.
Daughters with legs as long as this
lift and lift their thighs into the circle of desire,
hold sex on their lips like a prickly pear.

Sons get rid of love to have it
only to lose it again.

In this unimagined sun, sons and daughters
melt into their own lives.

Now comes the lantern of saying no,
the dark sun of goodbyes.

She tosses like useless vegetables.
"I am pieces of a person." Tears crash
from her cheeks,

the sea explodes like koolaide.
She is the end of a meal, the end of a disease
she can't get better from.

"Put a finger to my forehead. Blow out the candle."
He is a horse to her touch, huge and tamed.
She is a bird in his hands.

He recalls the pureness of unbroken voices,
boys before shorthairs ripen.
Emotions scatter his face like a wise baby.

He hears the bowlegged ladies call the tune
and is satisfied as a livingroom of grand pianos.
He understands

finally,
that the brain is a crowd
that the sea has no memory,
that the day is long that does not reach the night.

My everything are coming together, thinks he.
Now come grandchildren, thinks she.

Yes.

AGMV
MARQUIS
Québec, Canada
1999